23.95

SCIENCE HIGHLIGHTS

500–1500

MEDIEVAL SCIENCE

By Charlie Samuels

Gareth Stevens
Publishing

Please visit our Web site www.garethstevens.com. For a free color catalog of all our high-quality books, call toll free 1-800-542-2595 or fax 1-877-542-2596.

Library of Congress Cataloging-in-Publication Data
Samuels, Charlie, 1961-
Medieval science (500-1500) / Charlie Samuels.
    p. cm.
Includes index.
ISBN 978-1-4339-4139-9 (library binding)
ISBN 978-1-4339-4140-5 (pbk.)
ISBN 978-1-4339-4141-2 (6-pack)
1. Science, Medieval—Juvenile literature. 2. Technology—History—To 1500—Juvenile literature. I. Title.
Q124.97.S255 2011
509'.02—dc22

                    2010013222

Published in 2011 by
Gareth Stevens Publishing
111 East 14th Street, Suite 349
New York, NY 10003

© 2010 The Brown Reference Group Ltd.

For Gareth Stevens Publishing:
Art Direction: Haley Harasymiw
Editorial Direction: Kerri O'Donnell

For The Brown Reference Group Ltd:
Editorial Director: Lindsey Lowe
Managing Editor: Tim Cooke
Children's Publisher: Anne O'Daly
Design Manager: David Poole
Designer: Kim Browne
Picture Manager: Sophie Mortimer
Production Director: Alastair Gourlay

Picture Credits
Front Cover: Shutterstock: Fribus Ekaterina

Inside: iStockphoto: Kastelein 28; Bufi 45 (bl); **Public Domain:** 6, 9 (br); **Shutterstock:** Avalon 18; Cosma 11; Elen 42; Elena Elisseeva 29; fotohunter 32; Jaroslaw Grudzinski 43; Jeff Gynane 33, 44; Steffen Hoejager 15; Iagui 39; Inga Ivanova 9 (tl); Rich Koele 21; Philip Lange 24; Michael Levis 23 (tl); Macka 22; Anreas Meyer 30; Nikolay Okhitin 34; Andrew Park 13 (t); Route 66 23 (br); Tamara Rulikova 38; Stock 31; Tandem 19; Irina Tischenko 37; Titelio 20; Vesilvio 5; Nils Volkmer 14; Marco van Vurien 7; **Thinkstock:** Creatas 17, 35; Photos.com 8, 10, 26, 41, 45;

All Artworks The Brown Reference Group

The Brown Reference Group has made every attempt to contact the copyright holders. If anyone has any information please contact info@brownreference.com

Manufactured in the United States of America
1 2 3 4 5 6 7 8 9 12 11 10

CPSIA compliance information: Batch #CS10GS: For further information contact Gareth Stevens, New York, New York at 1-800-542-2595.

Contents

Introduction

The Middle Ages were a period of great advances in medicine, math, architecture, and technology as curious individuals tried to understand the world around them.

In the past, it was sometimes fashionable to see medieval science as little more than superstition and magic, full of alchemists searching for eternal life or trying to turn lead into gold. Today, historians understand that the Middle Ages were actually a period of great steps forward in both practical technology, such as the building of windmills to grind grain for food, and in theory, such as the development of mathematics and algebra.

Keeping Records

Classical knowledge recorded by the ancient Greeks and Romans virtually disappeared from Europe after the fall of the Roman Empire in 476. In the Islamic world, however, scholars preserved, translated, and spread this ancient learning. In China, meanwhile, paper was invented early in the period, eventually making it easier for discoveries to be recorded and passed on. Much technological development was gradual, with a series of tiny changes and adaptations leading over a long period of time to significant improvements to traditional tools or buildings. However, the spread of record keeping has also preserved the names of some individuals who made significant breakthroughs and discoveries.

About This Book

This book uses timelines to describe the developments in scientific knowledge and technology from about 500 to about 1500. A continuous timeline of the whole period runs along the bottom of all the pages. Its entries are color-coded to indicate the different fields of science to which the developments belong. Each chapter also has a subject-specific timeline, which runs vertically down the edge of the page.

Machines helped measure natural phenomena: this 1344 Italian clock showed not only the time, but also the phases of the moon and the positions of the sun in the zodiac. ⬇

Islamic Science

From about A.D. 750, science flourished under the Abbasid caliphs of Baghdad. Drawing on ancient Greek and Hindu texts, Muslim scholars also added their own discoveries.

 In this medieval illustration, the Persian physician Rhazes examines a patient.

TIMELINE
500-550

500 Cultivation of silkworms begins in Byzantium (now Istanbul), when Christian monks smuggle silkworms out of China.

520 The Roman philosopher Boethius translates many of the works of Aristotle from Greek into Latin, providing the main source of the works to later scholars.

500   510   520

KEY:

Astronomy and Math

Life Science

Engineering and Invention

500 In modern-day Ecuador, the Manteño people make thin copper ax heads, which they probably use as money.

510 Craftsmen at Gaza, in what is now Palestine, construct a complicated water clock that chimes to mark the passing of time.

Following the prophet Muhammad's return to Mecca in A.D. 630, followers spread his teachings throughout a vast empire from central Asia to Spain. The Muslims did not destroy cultures, but absorbed much from them. The rise of Islam saw an increase in learning.

↑ Mosques like this one in Damascus, Syria, were centers of learning and education.

Science and the Umayyads

Damascus was the first Muslim capital under the Umayyad Dynasty, but in 750 the Umayyads were overthrown and the capital moved to Baghdad under the Abassid caliphs. The seventh caliph, Abdallah al-Ma'mun, was one of the greatest. Around 820, he commissioned an astronomical observatory and library as part of the Bayt al-Hikma academy (The House of Wisdom). His astronomers calculated the angle between Earth's rotational axis and its orbital plane and his geometers calculated the circumference and radius of Earth. Their calculations were almost accurate.

Arabian alchemist Abu Musa Jabir ibn-Hayyan, (known as Geber), expanded the Greek idea that matter

Timeline

622 Muhammad's flight from Mecca to Medina

630 Muhammad's return to Mecca

750 Umayyad Dynasty overthrown; capital moves from Damascus to Baghdad under Abassid caliphs

c.820 Bayt al-Hikma (The House of Wisdom) established in Baghdad

c.830 Hindu numerals introduced

c.860 Medicine according to principles of Hippocrates practiced in Baghdad

c.880 Al-Battani (Albategnius) calculates the length of the year and the times of the equinoxes

c.900 Plaster of Paris used to support fractured bones

534 Japanese mathematicians begin using Chinese math.

542 An epidemic of bubonic plague breaks out in the eastern Mediterranean; within two years it kills a quarter of the region's population.

530   540   550

532 Isidorus of Miletus designs the domed church of Hagia Sophia in Byzantium (present-day Istanbul); it is now a mosque.

535 Chinese engineers build a machine for sifting flour; it uses a crank to turn rotary motion into back-and-forth motion.

Ptolemy, the Greatest

Astronomers in Arabia preserved the ideas of the Greek astronomer Ptolemy, which he set out in a book in A.D. 150. Ptolemy's admirers often called the book *Megiste* (greatest), and when it was translated into Arabic in about 827, it was given the Arabic *al* ("the") to make the title *Almagest*, by which it has been known ever since.

→ Ptolemy still influenced geography and astronomy many centuries after his death.

is made from earth, air, fire, and water. He believed the Greek elements combined to form sulfur and mercury, which could help make any metal, including gold. He experimented with varnishes, dyes, and the refining of metals.

Medicine and Math

Abu-Bakr Muhammad ibn-Zakariya al-Razi, or Rhazes, chief physician at the hospital in Baghdad, is said to have been the first person to note that measles and smallpox were different diseases. He left detailed notes so other scientists could learn from his work. Rhazes used plaster-of-Paris casts to hold broken bones in place. He may have been the first person to classify all substances as being animal, vegetable, or mineral.

Al-Khwarizmi (see box, right) continued the work of the Greek mathematician Diophantus of Alexandria, reading his works in the original Greek.

Islamic Astronomy

Most astronomers accepted the Greek Ptolemy's work, but around 880, Abu-Abdullah Muhammad

TIMELINE
550–600

550 In a book known as the *Book of the Golden Hall Master*, a Chinese author describes large, wind-powered carriages with sails.

550   560   570

KEY:

Astronomy and Math

Life Science

Engineering and Invention

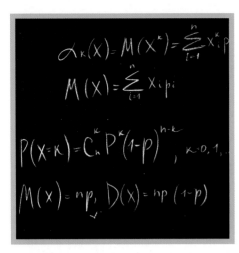

← Algebra was developed by Islamic scholars to solve complex math problems.

ibn-Jabir al-Battani, also called Albategnius, observed that when the Sun appeared at its smallest—when it is farthest from Earth—its position was not where Ptolemy said it should be. Albategnius worked out that the position changes slowly. This allowed him to measure the length of the year more accurately; calendar makers were still using his measurement centuries later.

The advance of Arabian science depended on scholars translating works from Greek into Arabic. One of the greatest translators was Honain ben Isaac, a Christian physician and philosopher living in Baghdad.

→ This stamp showing al-Khwarizmi was issued to mark his 1,200th birthday.

The Coming of Algebra

Arabic scholar Abu Jafar Muhammad ibn-Musa al-Khwarizmi studied Hindu and Greek math and used Hindu numerals in his works, which were later translated into Latin. He lived in Baghdad, where he was librarian at the House of Wisdom. In about 830, he wrote a treatise on math that was highly influential. In Latin, part of its title (*al-jabr*; "restoration") became "algebra." The Latin form of al-Khwarizmi's name—Algoritmi— also gave us our word "algorithm."

580   590   600

577 Chinese women invent a kind of match they use to start fires for cooking.

Making Paper

Writing is one of the greatest human inventions of all time. People needed something portable to write on. First was papyrus, then Chinese craftsmen invented paper.

↑ Egyptians wrote on rolls of papyrus, a kind of paper made from reeds.

TIMELINE
600–650

610 In India, mathematicians introduce a number system using base 10 (like modern math).

615 The Japanese use "burning water" as fuel: it is believed to have been petroleum.

622 This is the first year of the Muslim calendar, marking the Prophet Muhammad's flight from Mecca to Medina.

600   610   620

KEY:

Astronomy and Math

Life Science

Engineering and Invention

605 In Persia (modern Iran), farmers use windmills to grind grain; unlike modern windmills, the sails are horizontal.

610 The Chinese build the Great Stone Bridge over the Chiao Shui River using a segmented arch; the bridge still stands.

From about 2800 B.C., the Egyptians made papyrus—which gives us the word paper—from reeds growing along the banks of the Nile River. They peeled the reeds and sliced the inner pith into strips, which they criss-crossed and pounded into a flat sheet. Then they used smooth stones to polish the dried sheets of papyrus.

The Coming of Paper

Other early writing materials included tree bark, cloth, and thin animal skins made into parchment or vellum. Parchment is usually made from untanned sheepskins. It probably gets its name from the ancient Greek city of Pergamum in Asia Minor (modern Turkey) where it was made. Vellum is a similar, thinner material made from the skin of a lamb or calf. Workers clean the animal skin with lime, dry it on a frame to stretch it, and scrape it with a sharp blade to give it a smooth surface for writing on.

The first Chinese reference to paper comes in about A.D. 105 from the writer Ts'ai Lun, who was an official at the Imperial Court during the Han Dynasty (200 B.C.–A.D. 220). He describes making paper from rags and other materials, such as tree bark, although the process probably originated at least 100 years earlier. Chinese craftsmen also made paper from leaves and other vegetable matter. One

Timeline
2800 B.C. Egyptian papyrus

A.D. 105 Chinese paper

868 First printed book

960 Paper money in China

1150 First European papermill

1442 Printing press

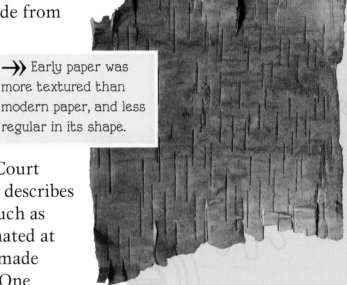

➤ Early paper was more textured than modern paper, and less regular in its shape.

635 Astronomers in China observe that the tail of a comet always points away from the sun; we now know the phenomenon is due to the solar wind, a stream of charged particles emitted by the sun.

630   640   650

628 Indian astronomer Brahmagupta writes a treatise on astronomy that also includes descriptions of complex math.

640 Paul of Aegina, a surgeon in the Greek city of Alexandria, writes "Seven Books of Medicine."

Making Paper

Papermaking has not changed much from how the Chinese made it in the first century A.D.
(A) Material such as leaves, mulberry bark, and bamboo shoots was pulped with water.
(B) The papermaker spread the pulp in a thin layer onto a fine screen or mesh.
(C) The water drained away to leave a crisscross of matted fibers that dried to form a sheet of paper.

➤➤ The Chinese invented papermaking in about A.D. 105. Today it is made by machine, but the principle is similar.

method involved taking young bamboo fibers and the inner bark of a mulberry tree and pounding them together in water. The resulting slurry was poured through a piece of cloth stretched on a wooden frame to act as a kind of filter. The water trickled through, leaving the fibers on the cloth, which dried to form paper. They also used hemp fibers in a similar way to make a finer grade of paper, but the most expensive kind was made from silk. Coarse paper was used as wrapping paper, while soft paper was used as toilet paper.

People in other parts of the world invented paper independently of the Chinese. Mesopotamians replaced their bulky clay tablets with a kind of reed paper resembling papyrus. By about the 6th century, inhabitants of the ancient city of Teotihuacán, Mexico, soaked and pounded fibers of fig bark to make paper. They coated it with a chalky varnish and then polished it with a smooth stone.

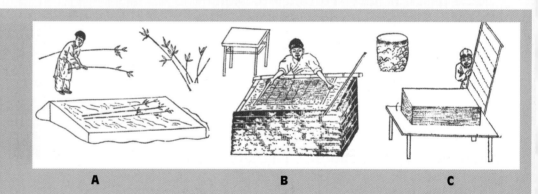

A   B   C

TIMELINE
650-700

650   660   670

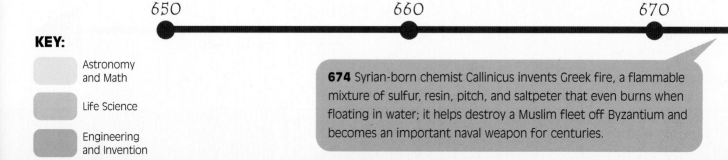

674 Syrian-born chemist Callinicus invents Greek fire, a flammable mixture of sulfur, resin, pitch, and saltpeter that even burns when floating in water; it helps destroy a Muslim fleet off Byzantium and becomes an important naval weapon for centuries.

In China and elsewhere, early paper could take the form of sheets or rolls.

Paper Spreads

Knowledge of papermaking spread from China to Korea, Japan, and Vietnam from the third to the sixth centuries, then to India and Samarkand in central Asia. By the eighth century, it had reached Damascus and Baghdad in the Middle East. Arab traders spread the technique to Egypt and northern Africa by the 10th century. They used flax (linen) fibers to produce very fine, strong paper. Later, grass fibers such as esparto, straw, and eventually wood pulp were used to make paper. The first European papermaking plant was built in 1150 near Valencia, Spain. Paper factories were now mills, either because waterwheels provided the power for the pulping machines or because grindstones were used to break up the vegetable materials.

Woodblock Printing

The earliest way of printing images used woodcuts, in which a design was cut in relief on the surface of a block of wood: unwanted wood was carved away. The printer applied ink to the raised surface, then squeezed the block onto a sheet of paper to transfer the image.

The image that appeared on the page was a mirror image of the original woodblock.

680 The Dutch build dikes to protect their low-lying land from the sea.

685 In Italy, the Ravenna Cosmography lists all the countries, rivers, and towns in the Roman empire.

691 The Dome of the Rock is completed in Jerusalem; it is made of wood and brass and covered in gold.

680

690

700

680 Mathematicians in Cambodia and Sumatra use the symbol 0 (zero) in calculations as a placeholder.

688 In China, empress Wu Tse commissions a 295-foot (90-m) pagoda constructed from cast iron.

Wind Power

The first windmills appeared in Persia (present-day Iran) in about 605. They were used to pump water into irrigation systems and to grind grain to make flour.

← These medieval windmills stand in the breezy La Mancha region of Spain.

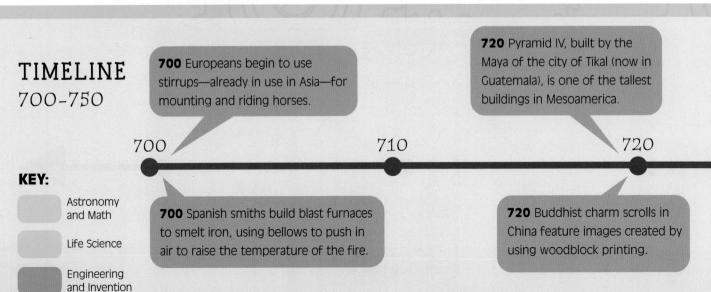

TIMELINE
700–750

700 Europeans begin to use stirrups—already in use in Asia—for mounting and riding horses.

720 Pyramid IV, built by the Maya of the city of Tikal (now in Guatemala), is one of the tallest buildings in Mesoamerica.

700   710   720

700 Spanish smiths build blast furnaces to smelt iron, using bellows to push in air to raise the temperature of the fire.

720 Buddhist charm scrolls in China feature images created by using woodblock printing.

KEY:

Astronomy and Math

Life Science

Engineering and Invention

Windmills arrived in western Europe in the 12th century—soldiers fighting the Crusades probably saw them operating in the Holy Land and brought the idea home. But early European windmills differed from early Persian devices (known as panemone windmills) in one important respect: Instead of being mounted on a vertical axis, European windmills had sails that radiated out from a horizontal axis, supported on the side of a post or a stone tower. This design makes much more efficient use of available air currents. On a vertical axis panemone, only half of the sails are exposed to the wind at any time, which means that at least half the available energy is lost. By mounting the sails on a raised horizontal axis, Europeans built mills that were immediately 100 percent more efficient.

It seems puzzling that the technologically advanced Persians did not figure this out, but a horizontal-axis windmill is, in fact, a much more complex device than a

In medieval Sweden, many farms had their own individual post mill, like this one.

Timeline

605 Panemone mills first operated in Persia

12th century Post mills appeared in Europe for grinding grain

1414 Mills used for drainage purposes in Holland

16th century Windmill technology introduced to the New World

1772 Spring sails invented

1854 Halladay mill patented

750 Arab scholars moving to Spain, now partly under Muslim rule, bring knowledge of the Alexandrine school to Europe.

730   740   750

725 Chinese engineer Liang Ling-Zan and Buddhist monk Yi-Xing build a water clock with an escapement mechanism to regulate its motion; it is not intended for timekeeping but to display various astronomical events.

750 Craftsmen in Italy use bronze to cast large church bells.

Where Does the Wind Come from?

The sun heats parts of Earth's surface to different temperatures. Because warm air rises, the difference in air temperature creates pressure differences. Wind is simply air moving from an area of high pressure to an area of low pressure. The larger the pressure differential, the stronger the wind. Windmills work best in places with a strong prevailing wind. Early millers understood this and tended to build their mills on flat plains, on the coast, or on top of small hills.

⟶ In a post mill, the structure could be turned toward the breeze. Inside, gears converted the force turning the horizontal shaft into a force for turning millstones around a vertical axis.

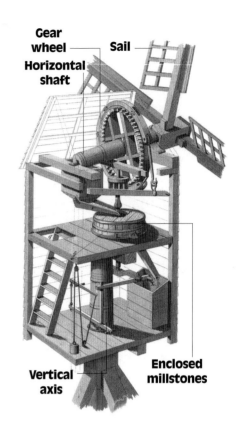

Gear wheel · Sail
Horizontal shaft
Vertical axis
Enclosed millstones

vertically mounted panemone. First, using an upright mill to turn millstones necessitated the use of gears to move the turning force through 90 degrees. For mill builders in Europe that was no problem, since the technology had already been invented for use with waterwheels. Second, an upright mill works effectively only if the sails are facing into the wind. Thus early European windmills were either built facing the prevailing wind—the direction from which the wind normally blows—or they had to be adjustable. The former solution worked well enough along the southern coasts of France and Spain and some Mediterranean

TIMELINE
750–800

750 The traffic of goods and ideas along the "Silk Road" peaks at this time; the network of routes connects China with Central and South Asia, and west to the edge of Europe.

770 The Arab scholar Abu Musa Jabir ibn-Hayyan, known in the West as Geber, describes how to prepare ammonium chloride, white lead, nitric acid, and acetic acid.

750   760   770

760 The use of "Arabic" numerals—they in fact came from India—reaches as far west as Baghdad.

774 Arabs begin to translate Hindu mathematical works into Arabic.

KEY:

Astronomy and Math

Life Science

Engineering and Invention

islands, where the wind nearly always blew off the sea, but farther north in Europe the winds were far too variable to make this a viable solution. So inland mills, known as post mills, were small and mounted on a single stout post that could be turned to face the wind.

Changing Direction

By the 15th century, windmill sails were mounted in a free-rotating cap that was separate from the main tower of the windmill. When the wind changed and the miller needed to adjust the direction the sails were facing, he only had to turn the cap, not the whole structure. This was usually done using a long pole that was attached to the back of the cap and angled down to the ground. The pole acted as a lever. Pushing the pole turned the whole cap. This advance meant that the size of windmills was no longer restricted by the need to turn them around. Mill towers could be built of brick or

↑ This traditional Greek windmill faces the prevailing breeze and can operate only when the wind blows from that direction.

789 Charlemagne, who rules a large empire in Europe, introduces standard weights and measures.

800 *Elements*, by the fourth-century B.C. Greek mathematician Euclid, is translated into Arabic.

780   790   800

780 Arabs in Baghdad learn how to make paper from Chinese craftsmen in Samarkand, on the Silk Road.

800 Metalworking techniques move north from South America into Central America.

The Halladay Mill

The Halladay mill, patented by U.S. machinist Daniel Halladay in 1854, played a key role in the settlement of the American West. It had a tail fin that automatically turned it to follow the direction of the wind. Thousands of such windmills still pump groundwater to the surface for livestock all over the rural United States and the Australian outback.

⟶ The invention of the Halliday mill revolutionized livestock farming in the United States.

stone, several stories high. Now windmills were proper buildings, rather than just machines. Building them taller meant they could have larger sails and therefore produce more power. There was also room for the miller and his family to live and work inside the building, with different stories for different tasks, such as storage, grinding, removing chaff from the milled flour, and bagging.

Spring Sails

To begin with, windmills used canvas sails mounted on wooden frames. The sails would be partially furled when the wind became too strong or taken off completely when the windmill was not in use. Then, in 1772, Scottish millwright Andrew Meikle invented spring sails. This marked a major change. Spring sails were made of wooden slats held shut by springs. When the wind blew hard, pressure on the sails

TIMELINE
800–850

800 In Arizona, the Hohokam people build a network of canals to irrigate their crops.

812 The Chinese begin to use bank drafts, the first form of money; the notes are known as "flying cash."

820 Arab mathematician Abu Jafar Muhammad ibn-Musa al-Khwarizmi describes the astrolabe.

800

810

820

KEY:

Astronomy and Math

Life Science

Engineering and Invention

800 Native Americans in the Mississippi Valley use the bow and arrow for hunting.

800 The Arab caliph Harun al-Rashid gives Emperor Charlemagne a water clock.

820 A scientific academy is founded in Baghdad; it is known as the House of Wisdom.

forced the sprung slats open so that they offered less resistance. This automation ensured that the sails turned at a steady speed however the wind changed, and allowed mills to operate in gusty conditions. Further improvements followed when, in 1807, English engineer William Cubitt invented a means by which the angle of the slats and thus the speed at which the mill turned could be adjusted while the sails were in motion. Being able to regulate the speed of the sails gave the miller much greater control over the quality of the flour he produced.

From Water to Electricity

Early windmills were used for just two purposes—pumping water and grinding grain. Nowhere were these roles more important than in Holland, where large areas of low-lying farmland were kept dry only by the constant activity of thousands of windmills that pumped out water from the fields. In the late 16th century, the invention of the crankshaft meant that windmills could also be to used to power sawmills. In Ohio in 1888, American inventor Charles Brush used a windmill to generate electricity.

↓ Early windmills were very simple: later mills were large enough for families to live in.

827 A second-century work by the Greek astronomer and geographer Ptolemy is translated into Arabic as *Almagest* (*The Greatest*). It is highly influential in the history of astronomy.

840 Arab astronomers record their first sightings of sunspots.

830   840   850

834 A manuscript illustrates the use of a hand crank to turn a wheel.

850 According to legend, coffee is discovered in East Africa by a goatherd named Kaldi.

Advances in Math

The European Renaissance revived learning. But the real revolution came with the invention of decimal fractions and logarithms in the 16th and 17th centuries.

→ The Chinese used the abacus for math calculations from about 1200 onward.

TIMELINE
850–900

KEY:

- Astronomy and Math
- Life Science
- Engineering and Invention

850 Arab physician Hunayn ibn-Ishaq writes a treatise about eye problems and their treatments.

860 Viking longships from Scandinavia sail as far west as Iceland, where Norwegians settle 14 years later.

855 A Chinese pamphlet—*The Classified Essentials of the Mysterious Tao of the True Origin of Things*—describes a "fire drug" (which seems to be an early form of gunpowder).

868 A Chinese printer creates the first printed book, a Buddhist work named *The Diamond Sutra*.

850 — 860 — 870

In 1142, English philosopher Adelard of Bath translated *Elements* by Greek mathematician Euclid, making the work available to Europeans, and the astronomical tables of Abu Jafar Muhammad ibn-Musa al-Khwarizmi, copying the use of Hindu-Arabic numerals. In 1145, English scholar Robert of Chester translated al-Khwarizmi's *Hisab al-jabr w'al-muqabala* (*Calculation by Restoration and Reduction*).

Italian Advances

It was Leonardo Fibonacci, an Italian mathematician, who explained how to use the new numerals in *Liber Abaci* (*Book of Calculation*), published in 1202. He first used a bar for fractions (¹/₄, for example). He wrote on geometry and on number series, including the series that bears his name, in which each number is the sum of the two preceding numbers: 0, 1, 1, 2, 3, 5, 8, 13, 21, and so on.

Timeline

1142 Latin translation of Euclid's *Elements*

1145 Latin translation of Al-Khwarizmi's *Hisab al-jabr w'al-muqabala*

1202 Fibonacci's *Liber Abaci* explains the use of Hindu-Arabic numerals

1494 Double-entry bookkeeping

1543 First popular English book on mathematics, *The Ground of Artes*

1585 Decimal fractions

1591 Use of letters to stand for quantities in algebraic equations

← Much early math was inspired by the need to record business dealings, like this later set of company accounts.

880 Arab astronomer Abu-Abdullah Muhammad ibn-Jabir al-Battani (known in the West as Albategnius) introduces trigonometry to Arab astronomy; he corrects the work of Ptolemy, calculates the length of the year, and determines the precession of the equinoxes.

880   890   900

876 In Gwalior, India, people use a symbol for zero as a placeholder in a number system.

→ The slide rule was invented in 1622 to help in calculations; it was still used 350 years later.

Scholars and Merchants

All the early works were written for scholars or merchants. English scholar Robert Recorde wrote the first popular English book on mathematics, *The Ground of Artes*. Published in 1543, it remained in print for over 150 years. Recorde was the first to use the equal (=) sign in 1557; plus (+) and minus (–) were introduced by German authors. Mathematicians wrote algebraic equations in words. In 1591, Frenchman François Viète wrote *In Artem Analytica Isogoge* (*Introduction to the Analytic Art*), using vowels to stand for unknown quantities, and consonants for known ones, producing the first equations that a modern mathematician would recognize. He is called the "father of modern algebra."

Meanwhile, in 1594 in Scotland, a brilliant mathematician named John Napier was busy devising a new method of calculation in which all numbers are expressed in exponential form. He called them "natural logarithms," meaning proportionate numbers, and in 1614 published tables of them.

A professor at Oxford University and a Napier admirer, Henry Briggs, pointed out it would be simpler to use 10 as a base. Briggs had invented "common" logarithms. In 1624, he published a

TIMELINE
900–950

900 Persian-born Arab physician Rhazes distinguishes between the diseases measles and smallpox; he also uses plaster of Paris to hold broken bones as they heal.

900   910   920

900 Arab chemists distill wine to make alcohol, which they use mainly in medicine.

KEY:

Astronomy and Math

Life Science

Engineering and Invention

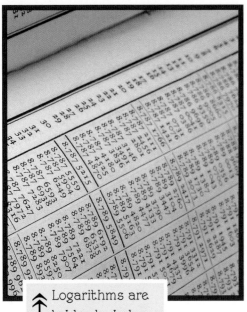

Logarithms are tables to help calculate complex math problems.

table of logarithms from 1 to 100,000. Briggs also invented the modern long division method.

Simon Stevin (also known as Stevinus), introduced decimal notation into math in 1585. Decimal fractions were only used over 30 years later, however, with Napier's adoption of the decimal point.

To speed up calculations, in 1617 Napier introduced a third innovation, known as Napier's "bones," or rods. They were straight sticks with a multiplication table carved on each one. The user arranged them in a lattice pattern to solve a calculation. The answer to any long multiplication became a matter of simple addition.

Around 1622, English mathematician William Oughtred invented the slide rule, which engineers and mathematicians used until the introduction of the calculator in the late 20th century.

→ This Italian coin was made to mark the 300th anniversary of Pacioli's breakthrough.

Luca Pacioli and Accountancy

In 1494, Italian monk Luca Pacioli, considered the founder of accountancy, invented double-entry bookkeeping and described it in his book *Everything about Arithmetic, Geometry, and Proportion.* Pacioli classed each transaction as both a debit and a credit to make sure the records balanced.

950 Arab settlers introduce the lemon plant to Sicily and Spain.

930   940   950

Castles and Bridges

After the Norman Conquest of Britain in 1066, fortresses sprang up across the country. Castles and fortified bridges continued to be built in Europe until the 14th century.

⇑ The White Tower of the Tower of London was built by the Normans in 1080.

TIMELINE
950–1000

960 In the Chinese province of Szechuan, paper money is printed and widely circulated as a means of exchange.

964 Arab astronomer Abd Al-Rahman Al-Sufi demonstrates the existence of the Andromeda Galaxy and the Large Magellanic Cloud.

967 An iron pagoda for a Buddhist temple is cast in sections at Guangdong, China.

954 The Chinese emperor Shih Tsung commissions a huge statue of a lion; at 44 tons (40 metric tons), it is the largest piece of cast iron ever made in China.

975 French cleric Gerbert of Aurillac builds a hydraulic musical organ.

950   960   970

KEY:

Astronomy and Math

Life Science

Engineering and Invention

Acastle is a fortified place. Originally built as strongholds for the kings or lords of the surrounding lands, castles were designed to be as safe from attack as possible. As the techniques and weapons improved for assaulting and laying siege to castles, walls were made thicker and higher. Castles also became larger to accommodate all the people and supplies needed to manage and sustain them.

Motte-and-Bailey Castles

When the Normans invaded England in 1066, they had to overcome resistance from local people living in castles built in a style found throughout Europe. The stronghold (keep), built of stone or wood, sat on top of a high mound, or motte, surrounded by a ditch. At its foot would be areas, called wards, protected by wooden palisades (fences made of stakes). This was known as a bailey, and so this is a motte-and-bailey type of castle.

Motte-and-bailey castles were used by the Normans in the early stages of their invasion of Britain. The artificial

← Motte-and-bailey castles had two parts. The motte was a mound with a wooden tower on top. The bailey lay at the foot of the hill, surrounded by a fence. It housed the townspeople.

981 One of the world's first hospitals is built in the Abbasid capital at Baghdad; it employs 24 physicians.

984 A Chinese writer describes the first use of canal locks.

1000 Viking longships reach North America.

980

990

1000

976 A Chinese engineer invents a chain-drive mechanism for a mechanical clock.

982 Viking longships from Iceland cross the North Atlantic Ocean to discover Greenland.

988 Persian astronomer Abu al-Wafa constructs a wall quadrant for observing the stars.

The Stone Keep

At the center of the castle lay the keep. This was the most heavily fortified part of the castle and the place to which defenders retreated if an enemy broke through the outer walls. The keep held the owner's living quarters and stores. It had a well and could withstand a long siege. In later castles, residential quarters were often in the bailey, leaving the keep as the last line of defense.

→→ The tall keep rises over Chepstow Castle, built on top of a sheer river cliff on the border between England and Wales.

→→ The keep's high walls prevented attackers from scaling the battlements.

earthen mound in the center of Windsor Castle dates from about 1075. The Normans also built castles of stone. The rectangular White Tower at the Tower of London dates from 1080. Castle walls varied in thickness, depending on the degree to which they were exposed to attack. Most were 6–7 feet (1.8–2.1 m) thick.

Building Baileys

One or more moats, sometimes with baileys between the moats, protected the castle's outer wall. Château Gaillard, on a cliff above the Seine River in France, has three baileys. The inner bailey is between the foot of the motte and

TIMELINE
1000–1050

1000 Indian astronomers introduce a calendar with 360 days divided into 12 months; an extra month is inserted every five years to keep the calendar in step with the seasons.

1006 Astronomers around the world observe a supernova that remains visible for months.

1000   1010   1020

KEY:

Astronomy and Math

Life Science

Engineering and Invention

1000 Persian physician Avicenna writes *Canon of Medicine*, a standard medical textbook for centuries.

1000 The Chinese begin to use coal as a fuel; soon they begin to mine it.

1021 Arab mathematician Alhazen publishes a treatise on optics in which he describes lenses and the refraction of light.

the inner moat, a middle bailey between the inner moat and the outer walls, and an outer bailey outside the walls but protected by the outer moat. The three baileys are in line, so an invader would have to take all three before reaching the keep. Richard I of England built Château Gaillard between 1196 and 1198, and in its day it was one of the best-protected castles in Europe.

Drawbridges crossed the moats, and the gateways were often protected by walled structures (barbicans) outside the main castle wall. As the drawbridge was raised, a portcullis (a screen made of wood and iron) could

Conwy Castle

Conwy Castle in Wales was built by English king Edward I as one of the key fortresses in his "iron ring," a series of strongholds built along the border to contain the Welsh. Instead of having concentric walls within walls for defense, Conwy towered up from an enormous natural rock, so it was virtually impossible to attack. Its thick walls contained eight huge towers.

⟵ This diagram includes a cutaway showing the main hall of the castle, which was used for eating and for entertainment.

1035 A hand-turned spinning wheel is introduced in China.

1045 Movable type made from baked clay is invented for printing in China; it is credited to a cloth seller named Bi Sheng. Within a decade, the invention is used for printing books.

1030   1040   1050

1030 In Italy, the Benedictine monk Guido d'Arrezo invents the first form of musical notation (for writing down music).

1044 A Chinese government official describes ballistic fire arrows, which are propelled by gunpowder.

The Krak des Chevaliers

Built by Christian Crusaders in what is now Syria, the Krak de Chevaliers is one of the most impressive medieval fortresses. Perched on a mountain spur that drops away on three sides, it occupied a strong defensive position. Its entrance was guarded by a complex series of twists and turns. The castle remained impregnable for nearly 130 years after it was built.

↑ The Krak des Chevaliers in Syria was built to defend Crusaders against local people.

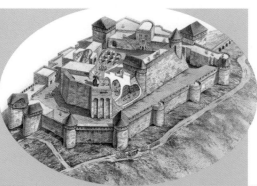

➔ Krak de Chevaliers had two widely spaced walls to reinforce its hilltop position.

be lowered so that it closed the gateway completely.

A castle displayed the wealth and power of its owner. After the English king Edward I suppressed the Welsh in 1282–1283, he built six castles to house his garrisons and to remind local people of his power. Caernarfon Castle, built between 1283 and 1322, still stands.

The Crusaders of the Middle Ages built many castles, one of the most impressive being the strategically located Krak des Chevaliers (castle of the knights) at Qal 'at al-Hisn, Syria. With an inner and outer wall separated by a wide ditch, it could hold a garrison of

TIMELINE
1050–1100

1050 Arab astronomers and navigators introduce the astrolabe into Europe.

1066 What is later known as Halley's comet is sighted in England; it is interpreted as an omen of the Norman invasion of that year.

1075 In Toledo, Spain, Arab astronomer al-Zarqali builds complex astronomical water clocks.

1050   1060   1070

KEY:

Astronomy and Math

Life Science

Engineering and Invention

1054 Astronomers in China and Japan record the sudden appearance of a supernova in the Crab Nebula that is visible in daylight for 23 days.

1075 In Italy, Trotula of Salerno works as an obstetrician, lectures at the university, and writes about female disorders—all very unusual for a woman at the time.

2,000 soldiers. The Knights of St. John (the Knights Hospitallers) built the castle and held it from 1142 until Sultan Baybars I captured it in 1271.

Decline of Castles

As castles grew bigger and stronger, so too did the artillery deployed against them. In the end, the guns were powerful enough to reduce any wall to rubble. Gradually the fashion for building defensive castles waned, and kings and lords built themselves palaces instead—for display and comfort, not for warfare.

↑ With three fortified towers, the Pont Valentré spans the Lot River in southern France.

Fortified Bridges of Europe

Bridges are such key defensive points that some, such as the 14th-century Pont Valentré at Cahors, southern France, were fortified. The bridge had three towers so defenders could keep traffic from crossing. Other bridges had shops, chapels, and other buildings all the way across. Old London Bridge was the first bridge with masonry foundations built on a swift-flowing tidal river—the Thames. Lined with houses and shops, it survived for more than 600 years.

1080 European farmers use the "swingletree" to allow two horses to pull a wagon or plow side by side.

1086 Shen Kua discusses earth science, including the principles of sedimentation, uplift, and erosion.

1080　　　　1090　　　　1100

1075 Arab astronomer al-Zarqali, also known as Arzachel, proposes correctly that the orbits of the planets are elliptical rather than circular.

1086 Chinese scientist Shen Kua describes a magnetic compass used for navigation.

1090 A Chinese minister builds a larger water-driven astronomical clock called the "Cosmic Engine."

Chinese Science

Some of the world's greatest inventions originated in China. Early Chinese scientists invented the kite, spinning wheel, compass, crossbow, and wheelbarrow.

↑ The Chinese enjoyed fireworks displays over 1,000 years ago.

TIMELINE
1100–1150

1100 After the invention of gunpowder, fireworks become popular in China.

1103 Chinese potters make a fine white ceramic called porcelain, which in Europe is called "china."

1120 Prior Walcher of Malvern Abbey, England, begins using degrees to express latitude and longitude on maps.

1100   1110   1120

KEY:

Astronomy and Math

Life Science

Engineering and Invention

1105 Persian mathematician and poet Omar Khayyam solves cubic equations (algebra equations of the degree 3).

1110 European military engineers invent the gravity-powered catapult.

1117 Chinese writer Chu Yu describes a compass used for navigation at sea.

C hinese general Meng T'ien is credited with inventing the camel's-hair brush as a tool for writing in 250 B.C. In those days, people wrote on cloth, but the popularity of the brush led to a demand for a cheaper and more plentiful medium. In about A.D. 105, Ts'ai Lun invented paper. The oldest-known printed book (a Chinese translation of the *Diamond Sutra*, a Buddhist text) is also Chinese, made in A.D. 868.

Chinese books on alchemy, also from the ninth century, contain formulas for making mixtures that burn with a flash: early gunpowder. In A.D. 132 a scholar, Chang Heng, invented an "earthquake weathercock." In fact, it was a seismograph.

Chinese Thought

Chinese and European thought developed along very different lines. Chinese thinkers had no key philosophical ideas, or theology. Each science was separate and produced partial and often indirect explanations for natural patterns and relationships that scholars believed were too complex to be fully understood.

Astronomy was very important because the Chinese believed the emperor must preserve a harmonious relationship with the cosmic order by living a pure and simple life and correctly performing rituals. This required a reliable calendar, based on astronomical

Timeline

1000 B.C. Kite

600 B.C. Iron plowshare

250 B.C. Camel's-hair brush

A.D. 1st century Rudder

A.D. 100 Wheelbarrow

c.105 Paper

132 Seismograph

868 First printed book

⬆ This Chinese compass used a lodestone (natural magnet) to indicate north and south.

1135 Scholars in Toledo, Spain, translate the medical works of Persian physician and philosopher Avicenna into Latin.

1140 Construction of a new basilica at the Abbey of Saint Denis begins in France; the building has a new form of supporting columns named flying buttresses.

1130

1140

1150

1126 Chinese military forces use gunpowder rockets and grenades in the defense of Kaifeng.

1140 King Roger II of Sicily introduces a system of government licenses that enable physicians to practice medicine.

1150 The first papermill in Europe is built in Valencia, Spain.

This early Chinese compass was used for feng shui, the practice of aligning buildings and rooms with key directions. It was only later that the compass was used for navigation.

observations. The present Chinese calendar emerged in the 14th century.

The calendar counted days, months, and years in cycles of 60. As well as marking the equinoxes, solstices, and agricultural seasons, the Chinese calendar contained the dates of predictable events. Irregular and therefore unpredictable events were seen as omens.

Chinese astronomers kept detailed records. From as early as the fourth century B.C., they noted the positions of stars in star tables, and there is a continuous record from about 70 B.C.

Chinese Math

Astronomy is a mathematical science, and the earliest-known Chinese mathematical text is the *Zhoubi Suanjing* (*Zhou Dynasty Canon of Gnomic Computations*), written sometime between 400 and 200 B.C. but based on much earlier texts that are now lost.

Early Chinese mathematicians noticed the relationship between a sound's pitch and the physical processes that produce it. This led to Chinese harmonics (used to tune stone chimes and bells used in rituals) and

TIMELINE
1150–1200

1150 In Spain, Arab physician Avenzoar introduces bloodletting as a medical treatment.

1155 The oldest-known printed maps are created in China, showing the west of the country.

1150

1160

1170

KEY:

Astronomy and Math

Life Science

Engineering and Invention

1150 Indian knowledge of algebra and arithmetic are summed up in *Siddhanta Siromani*.

1150 Hebrew astronomer Solomon Jarchus compiles the first celestial almanac, giving details about the stars.

1175 In Italy, Gerard of Cremona translates the *Almagest* of Greek astronomer Ptolemy from Arabic into Latin.

then to the development of court music. In 1978, archaeologists discovered 65 bronze bells with gold-inlaid inscriptions in a tomb from the 5th century B.C.

↑ The wheelbarrow appeared in China in about A.D. 100 for transporting goods.

Chinese Medicine

Chinese medicine, based on the cosmic principles of yin and yang, began about 2953 B.C. Much of Chinese medical literature is based on the text *Nei Ching*, traditionally attributed to the legendary Yellow Emperor, but more probably written in the third century B.C. Doctors relied mainly on the use of herbal, animal, and mineral substances. They used massage, physical and breathing exercises, and diet. The studies covered thousands of ingredients, increasing the Chinese people's knowledge of natural history.

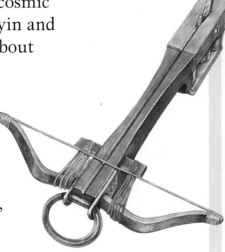

↑ Chinese emperors had thousands of crossbow archers in their armies.

The Crossbow

Crossbows were in use in China by the sixth century B.C. While conventional bows relied on the strength of the archer, the crossbow had a trigger, so that many bolts could be fired in succession without tiring the user. The greater tension on a crossbow string rather than a conventional bow string makes the bolt travel farther and penetrate even thick armor. The trigger also gave the crossbow great accuracy over a long range.

1180 European shipbuilders begin making ships steered by a rudder rather than by steering oars.

1193 Italian scholar Burgundio of Pisa translates the works of the Greek physician Galen into Latin; they have a huge influence on medicine for the following centuries.

1180   1190   1200

1180 Italian physician Roger of Salerno publishes *Practice of Surgery*, the first European book dedicated to surgery.

1185 Chinese jade workers invent the rotary disk cutter to cut the stone.

1200 Chinese mathematicians introduce a symbol for zero.

The Magnetic Compass

The development of the magnetic compass has its roots in China. But its branches bore the most abundant fruit when they spread into Europe in the Middle Ages.

◄◄ The magnetic compass was essential for navigation in the age of exploration.

TIMELINE
1200–1250

KEY:

Astronomy and Math

Life Science

Engineering and Invention

1205 In Spain, ironworkers improve the Catalan forge, a forerunner of the blast furnace.

1205 European farmers begin to grow buckwheat as an alternative cereal crop.

1217 Scottish scholar Michael Scot introduces the ideas of the ancient Greek scientist Aristotle into European astronomy.

1200   1210   1220

1202 Italian mathematician Leonardo Fibonacci introduces the Fibonacci series, a succession of numbers in which each number is the sum of the previous two.

1220 Universities are founded around now in Padua, Naples, Toulouse, Cambridge, and Rome.

The history of the compass and that of magnetism are closely linked. People knew about magnetism thousands of years ago, when they saw the unusual properties of certain rocks called lodestones rich in magnetite, a mixed iron oxide (Fe_3O_4), that is naturally magnetic. A shepherd named Magnus (magnet) discovered them when he noticed that the iron tip of his crook stuck to certain rocks.

Magnets and Navigation

Earth is a giant magnet. Its magnetic field is generated by electrical currents and convection currents in Earth's outer core. Earth's magnetic field has two poles: north and south.

By the first century A.D., lodestones were used in devices called south-pointers, used by Chinese mystics for astrology and fortune-telling.

During the eighth century, the lodestone in Chinese compasses was replaced by a magnetized iron needle. In 1086, Chinese scientist Shen Kua described a magnetic compass used for navigation. In 1117, Chu Yu's P'ingchow described the use of a compass at sea. But it was not until the age of European exploration that the device became a sophisticated navigational aid.

It was probably the Arabs who brought the compass to the West. Before that, European travelers used the

Timeline

1st century A.D. South-pointers (lodestones)

8th century Iron compass needles

11th century Vikings believed to use compasses at sea

1250 European sailors use portable compasses

1269 Compass dial

⬆ The Chinese used compasses to align buildings to achieve positive energies.

1240 A decree of the Holy Roman Empire permits the dissection of human corpses.

1240 English mathematician Johannes de Sacrobosco publishes *On the Sphere of the World*, a standard astronomical text for four centuries.

1230   1240   1250

1227 Japanese artist Kato Shirozaemon uses Chinese technology to start producing fine china in Japan.

1240 Arab physician Ibn al-Baytar lists 1,400 medications in a catalog of medicines and foodstuffs.

1242 English philosopher Roger Bacon gives precise instructions on how to make gunpowder.

Magnetic Deviation

Earth's magnetic north and south poles are not aligned with the true poles (the axis on which the planet spins). The effect is greater the closer you are to the poles. Things are complicated by the fact that Earth's magnetic field is not static. The positions of magnetic north and south drift slightly over time. But the movement is gradual, and can be easily compensated for when using a compass to give true directions.

→ Earth has its own magnetic field, which causes magnetic deviation.

sun or the polestar to show them north and south. They could achieve remarkable accuracy, but only with clear skies. Periods of bad weather made such navigation impossible, often with catastrophic results.

The Compass in Europe

The Vikings may have used compasses in the 11th century, but the first written reference to a magnetic compass in the West comes from *De Naturis Rerum* (*Concerning Natural Things*), published around 1180 by English scholar Alexander Neckam.

Early European compasses were not convenient for travel. By 1250, a needle was mounted on a pivot so that it hovered beneath a circular card marked up with the cardinal directions. When the needle moved, so did the card. A French scientist and soldier, Petrus Peregrinus, first described the laws governing the behavior of magnets (and hence of the compass) in 1269. He described magnetic poles and developed a compass dial, which allowed greater accuracy.

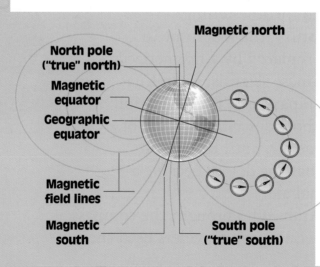

North pole ("true" north)
Magnetic equator
Geographic equator
Magnetic field lines
Magnetic south
Magnetic north
South pole ("true" south)

TIMELINE
1250–1300

1250 German monk Albertus Magnus isolates arsenic.

1262 Arab astronomer Nasir al-Din al-Tusi builds a well-equipped astronomical observatory at Maragheh, in present-day Iraq.

1250   1260   1270

KEY:

Astronomy and Math

Life Science

Engineering and Invention

1250 Armorers in Bohemia (in what is now the Czech Republic) make armor with tinplate, which does not rust.

1255 Carrier pigeons are used to carry messages in the Middle East—up to 400 miles (640 km) a day.

1269 French writer Petrus Peregrinus introduces the idea that a magnet has "poles" at either end.

Further refinements followed, including mounting the needle and dial inside a box made of wood or ivory, materials that did not interfere with the magnetic forces. Later models used brass for the same reason. In the 16th century, ships' compasses began to be mounted on self-correcting bearings, or "gimbals," that ensured the compass was always level despite the rolling of the ship.

An Indispensable Tool

Compasses became indispensable. In 1594, English philosopher Francis Bacon described the "needle" as one of the three most important advancements in the civilized world (the others being gunpowder and the printing press). As time went by, navigators realized that the compass needle was not infallible: It could be deflected by the proximity of certain objects, especially those made of iron. At sea, compasses could also be influenced by large landmasses; and when traveling east or west, navigators had to compensate for a phenomenon known as magnetic deviation.

↑ In this mariner's compass, the needle hovers from a pivot just below the dial, and the whole instrument is set inside a sturdy case that could be mounted on gimbals to keep it steady at sea.

1276 Italian physician Giles of Rome discusses the role each parent plays in procreation.

1290 In the Andes, people build cable bridges across deep gorges.

1280   1290   1300

1272 *The Alfonsine Tables*, the first astronomical tables prepared in Christian Europe, are published after 10 years' work.

1286 Eyeglasses are invented in Italy at about this time.

1300 False Gerber, a Spanish alchemist, describes sulfuric acid.

Clocks and Watches

The earliest timekeeper, used in ancient Egypt by about 3500 B.C., was a vertical stick in the ground that showed the time by the position of its shadow as the sun moved.

⟶ This 24-hour clock at the Capitano Palace in Padua, Italy, was built in 1344.

TIMELINE
1300–1350

1305 The hourglass is invented for telling the time.

1310 Portuguese sailors begin to make and use portolan charts to help with coastal navigation.

1316 Italian anatomist Mondino De' Luzzi publishes the first Western account of anatomy.

1300

1310

1320

KEY:

Astronomy and Math

Life Science

Engineering and Invention

1304 German scientist Theodoric of Freiberg investigates how raindrops form rainbows and discovers that refraction causes a colored spectrum.

1315 Spanish cleric Ramón Lull, or Raymond Lully, discovers ammonia gas.

1320 French surgeon Henri de Mondeville recommends the cleansing and stitching of wounds to aid healing.

By the eighth century B.C., the shadow clock had evolved into the sundial, with a triangular "fin" replacing the stick. Sand clocks also date from ancient times. The most common type, developed in the 14th century, was the hourglass, so called because it took one hour for dry sand to run from the upper section to the lower section. The British Royal Navy used hourglasses on board ships at sea until the 1820s.

Other Time Telling Devices

At night, when sundials naturally did not work, the ancient Egyptians used a water clock (clepsydra) to tell the time. The simplest consisted of a vessel full of water with a graduated scale marked on the inside. As water dripped out of the vessel through a hole in the bottom, the level on the scale inside showed the time. The Greeks added a float mechanism to move a pointer to indicate the time. Chinese inventors used mercury and water in their versions of a clepsydra.

In A.D. 725, Chinese engineer Liang Ling-Zan and Buddhist monk Yi-Xing made the first mechanical clock, based on the movement of a huge 33-foot (10-m) paddlewheel. Each "paddle" was a cup that filled with water and rotated the wheel by exactly one thirty-sixth of a turn. In about 1090, Chinese

⟩⟩ This portable sundial allowed travelers to tell the time on the move.

Timeline

725 First mechanical water-driven clock

996 Clock escapement

1380s Weight-driven clocks

1502 Spring-driven clock

1656 First pendulum clock

1675 Hairspring regulator

1333 Europe's first medieval botanical gardens is opened in Venice, Italy.

1336 Math becomes compulsory for all students at the University of Paris.

1345 Dutch engineers use windmills to pump water from low-lying land.

1330

1340

1350

1330 French Hebrew mathematician Levi ben Gershom invents the cross-staff, used as a navigational aid.

1340 The English start using avoirdupois weights (pounds and ounces), first used in France.

1346 The "Black Death" arrives in Europe; within four years it kills about a quarter of the population: 25 million people.

Verge-and-foliot Escapement

In a verge-and-foliot escapement, the verge was controlled by teeth (pallets) that engaged a crown wheel. As the foliot swung, a pallet disengaged the crown wheel, allowing the weight to fall and turn the hand. The foliot swung back, and a pallet engaged the crown wheel, stopping the fall of the weight. The foliot then swung in the other direction, allowing the weight to fall again.

⟫ The verge-and-foliot escapement was used to regulate clocks until about 1800.

imperial minister Su Sung built a huge water-driven astronomical clock, or "Cosmic Engine," which showed the apparent movement of the stars through the sky as well as the time.

The Mechanical Clock

The first mechanical clocks were driven by the action of a slowly falling weight at the end of a cord wrapped around a drum. At hourly intervals, a hammer rang a bell (there were no hands or dials). Our word "clock" comes from the German *Glock*, meaning bell. This type of clock is said to have been invented by the French cleric and scholar Gerbert of Aurillac in about 996, who later became Pope. Similar clocks dating from the 1380s still exist in cathedrals in France and England.

In 1502, German clockmaker Peter Henlein invented a spring-driven clock with a horizontal face and a single hour hand. In 1656, Christiaan Huygens, a Dutch scientist, designed the pendulum clock. The first one was made a year later by

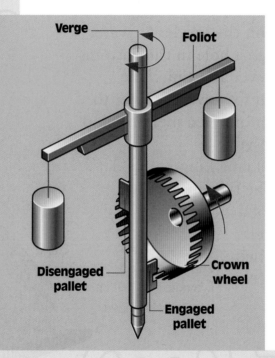

Verge

Foliot

Disengaged pallet

Crown wheel

Engaged pallet

TIMELINE
1350–1400

1350 Ironfounders in Liege, Belgium, make a blast furnace for extracting iron from its ore.

1363 French physician Guy de Chauliac describes how to treat fractures and hernias.

1350

1360

1370

KEY:

Astronomy and Math

Life Science

Engineering and Invention

1355 French philosopher Jean Buridan comes up with the idea of "impetus," which keeps celestial bodies continuously in orbit.

1364 Italian clockmaker Giovanni di Dondi makes an astronomical clock.

1377 Authorities at what is now Dubrovnik in Croatia use an island to quarantine travelers as a defense against the plague.

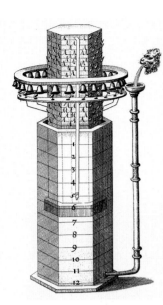

← This clepsydra, or water clock, used bells to chime the passing of the hours.

Salomon Coster in the Hague. English scientist Robert Hooke invented the anchor escapement in 1660. This device allowed the clock to release its energy gradually and regularly.

Henlein also made the first portable timekeeper, or watch, shortly before he died in 1542.

Spring-driven, it had an hour hand that showed through holes in the case. The oscillating balance wheel and hairspring regulator were invented in about 1675; they are still used today. In 1680, English clockmaker Daniel Quare made a watch that chimed the hours.

Anchor escapement

The anchor escapement was used in longcase clocks from about 1670. The swinging pendulum causes a horseshoe-shaped anchor to rock from side to side. The rocking motion allows the escape wheel to make a fraction of a turn at each half-swing. This action allows the driving weight to fall slowly, rotating the barrel and turning the hands of the clock.

← The anchor escapement regulated the action of a swinging pendulum.

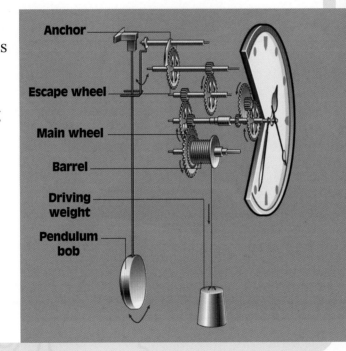

Anchor
Escape wheel
Main wheel
Barrel
Driving weight
Pendulum bob

1380 Military rockets are used in Europe for the first time at the Battle of Chioggia, between Genoese and Venetian armies.

1395 Chinese astronomers calculate the length of the solar year as 365.25 days (today's most accurate measurement is 365.242 days).

1380

1390

1400

1379 Italian writer Gabriel de Lavinde publishes a treatise on codes, which were in common use at the time (especially for diplomatic correspondence).

1391 The poet Geoffrey Chaucer writes the first technology book in English; it includes a description of a sextant.

1395 Printers in Korea use metal type.

Guns and Gunpowder

Gunpowder is a Chinese invention from the 11th century. The black powder and the firearms that used it would change the course of history across the globe.

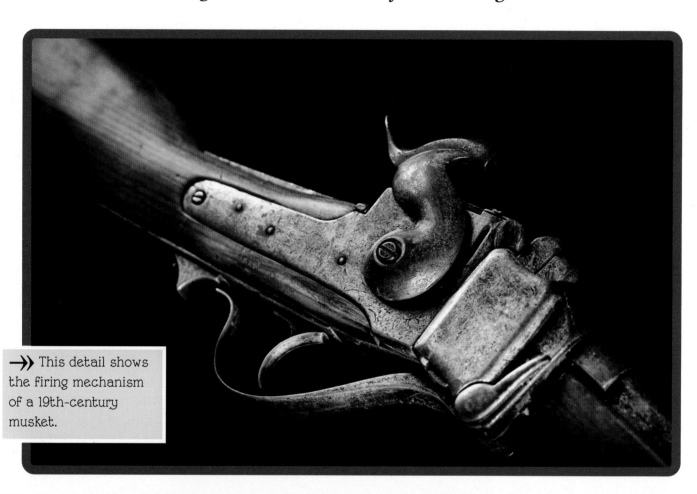

→→ This detail shows the firing mechanism of a 19th-century musket.

TIMELINE
1400–1450

1400 Dutch and Flemish artists begin to use oil-based paints.

1410 People in Ethiopia make coffee from the berries of the wild coffee plant.

1414 Fleets of large, oceangoing junks begin sailing from China to India, the Middle East, and as far as Africa.

1400

1410

1420

KEY:

Astronomy and Math

Life Science

Engineering and Invention

1405 Triangular lateen sails are used by Spanish sailors; they spread through the whole Mediterranean region.

1410 Hebrew astronomer Hasdai ben Abraham Crescas disagrees with Aristotle's theory that there are no other worlds except Earth.

1420 Filippo Brunelleschi begins building the dome of Florence Cathedral in Italy.

The origins of gunpowder are shrouded in mystery, mainly because the people who invented it wanted to keep it a secret. Gunpowder is a mixture of charcoal, sulfur, and saltpeter (potassium nitrate). When mixed in the correct proportions it burns rapidly, with 40 percent of the products being gases and the remainder solids in the form of smoke. The hot gases expand; if confined inside a container, they explode with a loud bang. If burned at the closed end of an open-ended tube, the expanding hot gases will push out a ball or bullet, which is the principle of the cannon and all firearms.

Early Steps with Gunpowder

With the advent of gunpowder, fireworks became popular in China in the 1100s. Fireworks often came in the form of strings of firecrackers; gunpowder bombs were more dangerous. Around 1220, the Chinese military made bombs with outer casings that shattered on explosion to kill or maim the enemy. A Japanese woodcut of 1292 illustrates a bomb exploding, showing that gunpowder had reached Japan by then. There is a reference to saltpeter and rockets in a 1280 book on warfare from Syria.

The gunpowder cannon turns up in the late 1280s,

⟩⟩ This pair of ornate flintlock pistols were made from brass and wood.

1425 German cleric Nicholas of Cusa suggests that Earth rotates on its axis every day and orbits the sun once a year; he anticipates by 100 years the similar theories of Polish astronomer Nicolaus Copernicus.

1445 Portuguese shipbuilders develop the caravel design; the sturdy caravel will be used by many navigators over the next two centuries, including Christopher Columbus.

1430   1440   1450

1430 The matchlock is introduced as the firing mechanism for small arms.

1442 German inventor Johannes Gutenberg sets up a printing press using movable type, the first in Europe.

1450 European metalworkers learn to separate silver from lead ores such as galena.

Berthold Schwarz

Berthold Schwarz was a famous semi-legendary character of the 14th century. He is often said to have been a monk and alchemist who lived in Germany in about 1320. He was said to have been nicknamed Schwarz ("black") because of the thick smoke surrounding his primitive chemical experiments, and he is credited with the invention of gunpowder in Europe. The composition of the explosive was first described in writing in Europe by English scientist Roger Bacon (c.1214–1292) in 1242.

↑ A war reenactor fires a matchlock musket by using a fuse to light the powder.

when the Chinese military used them. Around 1300, Arab technicians made cannon barrels from bamboo tubes. Metal barrels made from a bundle of wrought-iron rods were bound with iron. In 1346, the English used wrought-iron cannons, called bombards, against the French, and a year later European gunsmiths made arrow-firing cannons. German gunsmiths cast the first cannon barrels as a single piece of bronze in 1378. Bronze was chosen, especially for ships' cannons, because it does not corrode as easily as iron. French gunners used cast iron to make cannonballs from about 1495, and cast-iron barrels were first made in England in 1543.

Personal Weapons

The first "small arm" was invented in Spain in the mid-1400s. The shooter propped the barrel on a support, firing the weapon from the shoulder. The gunpowder

TIMELINE
1450–1500

1451 German cleric Nicholas of Cusa prescribes eyeglasses with concave lenses for nearsighted people.

1457 The first passenger coach, with suspension, is built at Kocs in Hungary (and named after the town).

1464 German mathematician Regiomontanus writes an overview of trigonometry.

1450   1460   1470

KEY:

Astronomy and Math

Life Science

Engineering and Invention

1453 At the Siege of Constantinople (now Istanbul), Ottoman forces employ a huge cannon that fires cannonballs weighing up to 1,345 pounds (610 kg).

1461 Breech-loading cannons are first used in Europe.

1473 In Italy, the first European version is published of *The Cannon of Medicine* by the Persian physician Avicenna.

charge was put in the barrel and lit with a matchlock. The musket replaced this within a hundred years and the flintlock replaced the matchlock.

To fire a flintlock, the musketeer first poured gunpowder down the muzzle, then a lead ball. He rammed a felt wad in to keep the ball and charge in place. He then put some fine powder in the pan at the side of the lock, and pulled back the cock, which held a piece of flint. As he pulled the trigger, the flint hit the steel and made sparks that ignited the powder in the pan. This lit the main charge, and the musket went off.

↓ From 1543, cannons were made of cast iron, reducing the risk of the barrels exploding.

The musket had a smooth bore; it gave way to the rifle, which had a spirally grooved barrel to give a spin to the ball or bullet. Further developments led to the breech-loading rifle and cartridges. Handguns followed the same pattern, going from muzzle-loading flintlock pistols to cartridge weapons. Another advance was the introduction of multishot revolvers.

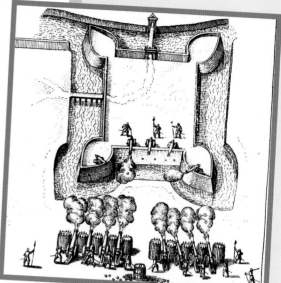

↑ This illustration from the 17th century shows cannons being used to besiege a fortress. As cannons improved, so the design of defenses improved— in turn inspiring further improvements in weaponry.

1482 Italian mathematician Johannes Campanus translates *Elements*, by the ancient Greek mathematician Euclid, into Latin.

1492 Italian navigator Christopher Columbus sails across the Atlantic to islands in the Caribbean.

1480   1490   1500

1485 Italian artist and inventor Leonardo da Vinci produces a design for a parachute.

1494 Italian mathematician Luca Pacioli describes double-entry bookkeeping: it is the basis of all modern accounting.

1496 England's King Henry VII establishes the length of the standard yard and sets other weights and measures.

Glossary

alchemy An early form of chemistry; alchemists tried to cure all diseases and to turn base metals into gold.

algebra The branch of mathematics that studies the properties of mathematical structures, and in which unknown quantities are denoted by letters.

astrolabe An early navigational device for measuring the height of the sun, from which the time could be calculated.

astronomy The study of objects outside Earth's atmosphere.

compass A navigational device with a pivoted magnetized needle that always swings to point to magnetic north.

escapement In clocks and watches, a mechanism that controls the regular release of energy from a falling weight or coiled spring.

flintlock A mechanism used to ignite the charge in a muzzle-loading pistol or musket; the trigger produces a spark from the flint, which ignites the charge.

gears Toothed cogs used to transmit rotary motion from one part of a machine to another.

geometry The branch of mathematics that studies the properties of shapes.

gunpowder An explosive mixture of powdered carbon (charcoal), saltpeter (potassium nitrate), and sulfur.

lodestone A piece of the mineral magnetite, which has magnetic properties (it attracts iron or steel).

magnetic north The direction indicated by the needle of a compass; it is not quite the same as true north.

matchlock A type of early firing mechanism for a musket, using an S-shaped piece of metal holding a fuse.

optics The science of light and vision.

portolan chart An early European navigational chart showing coastlines and place-names.

Renaissance A cultural movement (the word means "rebirth") that began in Italy in the 14th century and spread through Europe by the 16th century.

trigonometry The branch of mathematics that deals with angles and triangles.

waterwheel An early device to harness the energy of flowing water.

Further Reading

Books

Brezina, Corona. *Al-Khwarizmi: The Inventor of Algebra.* New York: Rosen Central, 2005.

Brocker, Susan. *Paper Trail: History of an Everyday Material.* New York: Children's Press, 2007.

Collier, James Lincoln. *Gunpowder and Weaponry.* New York: Benchmark Books, 2003.

Greenberger, Robert. *The Technology of Ancient China.* New York: Rosen Central, 2006.

Hibbert, Clare. *Look Around a Medieval Castle.* Mankato, MN: Arcturus Publishing, 2007.

Kelly, Jack. *Gunpowder: Alchemy, Bombards, and Pyrotechnics: The History of the Explosive that Changed the World.* New York: Basic Books, 2005.

Levy, Janey. *Keeping Time Through the Ages: The History of Tools Used to Measure Time.* New York: PowerKids Press, 2004.

Ryles, Briony, et al. *Medieval Period and the Renaissance.* Redding, CT: Brown Bear Books, 2010.

Trueit, Trudi Strain. *Gunpowder.* New York: Children's Press, 2005.

Web Sites

http://www.al-bab.com/ arab/ science.htm
Al-Bab page on Islamic science, with history and biographies.

http://www.historyforkids.org/learn/ china/science/
History for Kids page on Chinese science.

http://www.indepthinfo.com/ windmills/history.htm
InDepthInfo page on history of windmills.

http://cybersleuth-kids.com/sleuth/ Math/History/index.htm
Cybersleuth Kids page with links to subjects about the history of math.

http://www.historyforkids.org/learn/ medieval/architecture/castle.htm
History for Kids page on castle design.

http://www.historyworld.net/ wrldhis/PlainTextHistories.asp? historyid=ac08
A history of clocks from History World.

Index